Quit Making Excuses & Loc Your Hair

Quit Making Excuses & Loc Your Hair

EXPLORE MY LOC HAIR JOURNEY

C. Michelle Greene-Smalls, MSN, RN, CCM

QUIT MAKING EXCUSES & LOC YOUR HAIR
Explore My Loc Hair Journey
©2021 by C. Michelle Greene-Smalls

ALL RIGHTS RESERVED

This book is based on a true story. Some of the names and characters may have been changed to protect the privacy of the people involved. The events described in this book are written from the author's perspective, and as such are deemed to be a true representation from the author's point of view.

No part of this publication may be reproduced, stored in or introduced into a retrieval system, or transmitted in any form or by any means electronically, mechanically, or by photocopying, recording, or otherwise, except for brief quotations in printed reviews, without prior written permission from the author or publisher.

ISBN 978-1-7377290-8-2

For more information on the content of this book,
email cgreenesmalls@gmail.com

JMPinckney Publishing Company, LLC
104 Berkeley Square Lane
PMB 28
Goose Creek, South Carolina 29445

First printing December 2021/Printed in the United States of America

This book is dedicated to my mother, Cherrie, to whom I declared as a little girl that I'd write a book one day. Here it is. Your memory and love are with me always.

For you created my inmost being; you knit me together in my mother's womb. I praise you because I am fearfully and wonderfully made; your works are wonderful, I know full well.
Psalm 139:13-14

I can do all things through Christ who strengthens me.
Philippians 4:13

Table of Contents

Introduction xi
Chapter 1 Chemicals 1
Chapter 2 Desire for Long Pretty Hair 5
Chapter 3 Natural by Choice 9
Chapter 4 Peer Support 12
Chapter 5 Natural Hairstyle Options 14
Chapter 6 Loc Myths 22
Chapter 7 Starting the Locs 24
Chapter 8 Loc Maintenance Routine 28
Chapter 9 Interesting Things I Didn't Know Before
Starting Locs 35
Chapter 10 Mistakes With My Locs 38
Chapter 11 Loc Acceptance 42
Chapter 12 Easy Do It Yourself (DIY) Styles 48
Afterword 61
About the Author 62

Introduction

You're probably on the fence about starting locs, also known as dreads. I was too. It took me years of internal debating and then I finally did it.

I feel like you should, too. Do you want to know why? Because you are just wasting time. You won't know what it's really like until you try. Quit worrying about your hair type. Whether your hair is fine, soft, or coarse, you can start your locs!

In this book, I'll share with you how I got started. This includes my hair journey from a kid with all kinds of chemicals applied to my hair to a grown woman with locs near my waistline. You're going to learn about the mistakes I've made, how to maintain your locs, and how to do some simple hairstyles yourself. I've had my locs for 9 years. It's one of the best decisions I've made.

CHAPTER 1

Chemicals

Growing up, my hair was referred to as "nappy" and "peezy". This came from adults and kids. It was nothing to be proud of back then. Those were terms to surely be teased about. On some occasions, the adults would use the term "coarse". That didn't sound too bad to me.

Chemicals were introduced to my hair at a very young age. I want to say probably at age five. The first chemical was called the Jheri Curl. The Jheri Curl was popular in the 1980s and that's exactly when I got the chemical placed in my hair. It wasn't done in a salon, but by a lady in the neighborhood at her home. Yes, I said at her home. I believe my mother wanted to try this option to help manage my hair care. In other words, make it easier to comb and help it to grow. Needless to say, that Jheri Curl didn't last long. Why? I'm not exactly sure.

Without chemicals, my hair could be described as tough. Since the Jheri Curl was unsuccessful, the next thing was the relaxer. The purpose of the relaxer is to eliminate the kinks in your hair. The chemicals would make your hair straight by altering your natural curl pattern. By getting a relaxer, it was intended to make your hair easier to comb. When it comes to beauty, the relaxer's purpose is to make your hair more European-like. The relaxer was also interchangeably called a perm. Trust me, I had every relaxer that was available. Let me go down the list. The relaxers were: Dark N Lovely, Soft & Beautiful, Precise, Optimum, Just For Me, TCB, PCJ, and Ultra Sheen. It's probably more than that. I just can't recall. Then there was also the popular kiddie kit. It was deemed not as strong as a chemical, but suitable for children. However, every relaxer purchased for me was labeled, super, coarse, or extra course.

The relaxers that I just mentioned were accessible via the shelves of emporiums, such as Walmart, Kmart, Family Dollar, and beauty supply stores. The relaxers came in a small square or rectangular box with a pretty little Black girl or woman on the outside. Inside the box was a round plastic container filled with a white cream, which is the actual relaxer. The relaxer is sometimes referred to as "creamy crack". It's a term coined by comedian, Chris Rock, in his movie, *Good Hair*. Other essential items were in the box too. There were at least two small bottles filled with shampoo and neutralizer, a chemical-filled packet to mix inside the creamy crack, a small wooden stick in the shape of a tongue depressor or a fat popsicle stick, and thin plastic gloves. Now that I think about it, this was indeed a science project. My mom would buy them and mix the creams and chemicals herself and apply it to my hair.

Instructions were included with the relaxer as well. I recall my mother parting my hair with the comb into four sections starting from ear to ear and my forehead to the nape of my neck. Then the relaxer would be applied to the roots of my thick hair. If I'm not mistaken, the relaxer would stay on my hair for about 30 minutes. The next step was rinsing the hair to remove the relaxer. Afterwards, the hair would be shampooed. If the neutralizing shampoo turned pink after the relaxer was rinsed out, that was an indication of the relaxer still being present. Sometimes, this took several rounds shampooing to ensure all of the relaxer was completely out of the hair. Once the shampoo turned white, you were good to go. Finally, it was time for the conditioner application. Depending upon the brand, it was either a leave-in or conditioner requiring a rinse after a few minutes.

Nothing is relaxing about the relaxer. Frequently, I'd experience burning sensations on my scalp. Again, the goal was to keep the relaxer on my hair for 30 minutes. Often times the burning would become unbearable. I can remember squirming in the kitchen chair because the relaxer felt so hot on my head. You'd want the relaxer to stay on your hair so the relaxer would "take". In other words, if the relaxer "took", then you have achieved success by obtaining straight, non-kinky hair. There were interventions implemented to help me keep the relaxer applied for 30 minutes. Cooling methods included fanning my head, applying cold water, or hair spray to the burning areas. I'd get words of encouragement as if I were running a marathon like, "just a little longer" and "you're almost done." Distraction by watching television was used too. If the interventions failed, the relaxer would be rinsed out to provide relief.

Although these were actual chemicals on the hair, sometimes the relaxer would accidentally get on the skin of my forehead, neck, and ears. Eventually, the relaxer would damage the skin and scabs would soon form. The break in skin wasn't very noticeable. It depended upon how my hair was styled. There were times when I'd see the "white meat" that comedian, Bernie Mac, used to reference.

There were rare occasions in which I went to a hairdresser, also known as a beautician or cosmetologist. The hairdressers had their own relaxers that they used. I'm not sure of those names. The hairdressers recommended that relaxers be applied every six weeks. However, those relaxers weren't very effective either. My hair wasn't silky smooth and straight for very long.

Why were they not effective? I'm going to say it's because harsh chemicals such as relaxers don't belong on your hair. I already mentioned that the relaxer burns your scalp, it can cause skin irritation, and your hair can be damaged or even fall out. Do ya'll remember the episode on the television show, *Martin,* when Gina was in charge of doing Myra's relaxer? I haven't seen or known anyone's hair to fall out exactly like that, but anything is possible.

I believe wholeheartedly that relaxers contribute to uterine fibroids and reproductive issues. For those unfamiliar with the term uterine fibroid, it's a non-cancerous tumor located inside or around the uterus. Women can have several at a time. Trust me on this. Doctors don't know exactly why uterine fibroids develop. It could be related to hormones, hereditary factors, etc. Many Black women develop them. White women get them too, but at a much lower rate. What's one thing that most Black women have in common? The answer is relaxers. Now, that has been my own personal theory. However, a study completed by the [American Journal of Epidemiology](#) in 2012, concluded there is in fact a correlation between uterine fibroids and relaxers.

CHAPTER 2

Desire for Long Pretty Hair

As a kid, my hair was really short. There were a few little girls in the neighborhood with really long, thick hair that fell down their backs. However, there were no girls or no one in my family who had extremely long hair. My mom's hair was short, and her mother's hair was short too, so I was comfortable with my hair being short.

I do recall in first grade having a desire for long hair, but I wasn't wishing on a star or anything like that. Plenty of girls in my class didn't have long hair. There may have been one or two who did. My best friend's hair at the time was even short. It was other adults' perceptions that triggered me.

The first graders at my school were participating in a *Cinderella* stage play that was held at the school. The roles were dispersed and somehow I was selected as the moderator. At six years old I didn't know what that was. I just wanted to be active in the play. I even wondered why I couldn't have been Cinderella. Now that's confidence at an early age.

The play was held that evening after school was dismissed. I showed up in my blue and white polka dot dress that my Grandma sent me from New York and did my part. I stood before the crowd and gave the details of what was to occur throughout the scenes. When Cinderella came out, I was in awe of how pretty she looked, but still wondered why I couldn't have been Cinderella. I knew I could learn the lines. I wanted to look like a princess. I wanted to wear a crown, and a pretty poofy dress with fancy creative shoes. Y'all know the story of the glass slippers right? I said creative because our teachers used aluminum foil to cover the shoes to make them look like glass.

I'm a very logical thinker to this day and I applied some logic to this situation. The crowd just "ooohed" and "ahhhed" when she came out. I thought to myself, it had to be that she had the long pretty hair down her back. Don't get me wrong, there was no jealousy. I was a child and this was a pivotal moment where my understanding of what adults deemed as beautiful came to fruition.

There's a picture of me in first grade with several weave cornrows that formed into two long pigtails touching my shoulders. I was as happy as could be smiling with multiple teeth missing. I'm quite sure after the *Cinderella* play that my mom tried to make me happy by adding more hair to my head so I would have more length.

By fifth grade, I started styling my hair. This was just simply one or two ponytails. My hair was about shoulder length now. At this time I was happy if all of my hair would hold into one ponytail. When I say "hold", I mean hoping none of my hair in the back or side would fall. Sometimes, I used hair clips to hold the hair in place. Then again, sometimes that didn't work. Another thing I'd do was go to the sink to wet my hair. To do that I'd cup some water in my hand and place it on my hair. Then I'd grab the comb and brush. After that, I'd place my hair in a scrunchie for a ponytail.

By sixth grade, things were getting a little different. This was the beginning of middle school. Here, I'm faced with attending a new school and new students, whereas I knew everyone in 5th grade classes at my old school. Sixth grade marked where I started getting more braid extensions. Braids were the only type of weave I was allowed to get.

The weaves for braids were cheap. The hair was synthetic and it cost about 69 cents a pack. Some styles with synthetic hair were box braids, cornrows, Dookie braids, French braids, and Goddess braids. This was a time when you had to burn the ends of the braid with a cigarette lighter. Once the ends were burnt, they were dipped in a cup of water. This method would seal the ends. Thankfully, things have changed today where this method is nonexistent.

During this era, the French Roll was popular too. I wanted one really badly. One particular time, my cousin's mother was getting married. I was in the wedding as a junior bridesmaid. The junior bridesmaids got French Rolls for their hairstyle. Guess who didn't get one? Me! Maybe because I didn't have enough of my own hair. I don't know, but I was definitely mad. There's a picture of me somewhere with a "not so happy" facial expression when the style was completed. Tell me why I would be excited for a tiny ponytail with a bang in the front and back. My mom could've done that instead of me going to a hairdresser.

Speaking of ponytails, when Mary J. Blige's video for her song, "Real Love" came out, I was in love with her hairstyle. She had a big curly ponytail with strands of hair hanging down from the top of her hair. Of course, I wanted that style. That style required additional weave tracks. My mom wasn't about to purchase that kind of hair for me. Tracks are types of weave that come in packs and when you open them, it spreads horizontally like a curtain. The tracks back then were primarily glued to your hair or scalp. Hair glue was used, not Gorilla Glue.

As you can see, when it comes to hair, I've been influenced by trends and television at a young age. Today social media, is a big influence on many young people. Black children need to have a strong sense of self when it comes to hair. I'd say to parents of children, tell your daughters and sons that their hair is beautiful the way it is. Nothing needs to be added. Whether kinky or straight hair, the hair should be healthy.

CHAPTER 3

Natural by Choice

Natural hair is considered hair in its natural state without any chemicals such as perms, relaxers, texturizers, and dyes. I don't mind hair coloring now and then, but technically that's considered to not be natural. However, if you haven't had your hair relaxed for more than 6 months, I'd say you are natural.

Why did I become natural? I figured you'd want to know. I decided to bow out of the relaxer creamy crack game. I was forced out actually. All my little money went to bills as I was working part-time and going to nursing school. Since I wasn't making a lot of money, going to the cosmetologist was definitely a luxury that I couldn't continue to afford. Instead, my mom would do the box relaxers for me. However, one day I took matters literally into my own hands. I was fed up with basically needing a relaxer every 2 weeks (I didn't apply a relaxer every two weeks, but based on the way my hair looked I probably needed one more frequently than the recommended 6 weeks). I bought a box relaxer and applied it myself. In a desperate attempt to keep my hair straight for a longer period of time, I applied the creamy crack from the root of my thick hair to the ends! All of my hair was covered with the relaxer.

Like I said before, the relaxer came with instructions. If you didn't follow the instructions carefully you could potentially cause more damage to your hair. Well, covering all of your hair is not part of the instructions. After shampooing and conditioning my hair I still didn't know right away that damage was done. It probably took me a couple of months to figure out that my hair was not healthy.

I vividly remember pulling my hair back into a ponytail for work. The ponytail was so thin, but it was long. I was pleased with the length and became very satisfied with that. Then I had an "aha moment" recalling that my hair used to be thicker and fuller. This was the straw that broke the camel's back. I decided that was my last relaxer.

In 2002, I gave up relaxers. A professional cosmetologist recommended that I cut my hair, so I got my hair cut. The haircut was a result of hair damage in various parts of my hair. I wore my hair in a short, stacked style, resembling Halle Berry's hairstyle. Then I let the hair continue to grow out from there. When my hair started growing in its naturally curly state, I realized my hair was jet black! Not dark brown. My hair looked and felt like cotton. I was in awe.

CHAPTER 4

Peer Support

There was little support during the natural phase. YouTube wasn't created yet. I'd heard of *Nappturality*, a website for natural hair women from an agency nurse at work. Amber was older than me, but she kept me inspired. Occasionally I'd browse the site; however, I was doing my own thing.

When I started going natural in my early 20s, not having a relaxer was kind of taboo. It was frowned upon by some family members. They couldn't understand my wanting to be natural. They recommended other relaxers, trying another stylist, etc. My cousin who cut my hair actually recommended another relaxer for me to try. I had other cousins and friends who were quick to say that they couldn't be natural. Fast forward to today, they are natural with either locs or just relaxer-free. Today I can say that all of my friends who I've known since school or college have been delivered and are relaxer-free! Won't He do it!

In your 20s is where you begin to start to figure out who you are. I was a struggling nursing student, determined to graduate to make a better life for myself. I was trying to appreciate my physical looks, despite my skinny stature. I was also hoping to meet a good guy that I could eventually settle down with as well.

With that being said, as my hair was transitioning, I was concerned about being deemed attractive to the men. I'd never seen any girls in school or college wear their hair naturally. Unless they had the soft curly hair they were born with. They all had relaxers or weaves. Initially in my mind, I thought the men wouldn't find natural hair attractive. I just figured the little attention that I was getting from the guys would diminish even more if I wore my natural hair. I'm talking about kinky 4C hair like mine. Little did I know, I was beginning to start a revolution.

Believe it or not, I ran into men that liked my hair styled in its natural state. They were young and old. Again, I became natural for me, but it didn't hurt that the guys liked the new look too. When I met my husband, I had on my wig. After a few dates, I let him know the wig wasn't my real hair. He was shocked. I showed him my real hair and told him this is how I'm choosing to wear my hair. I told him if he didn't like it, we can call it quits because I'm not changing. He didn't mind it though.

My hair has been natural for almost twenty years. Today, I'm not concerned with ever having straight hair again. It just doesn't look right on me. At all! The natural hair state is a lifestyle for me. I've come too far and I won't turn back.

CHAPTER 5

Natural Hairstyle Options

Wigs

Wigs became my friends. I chose to wear wigs for a few reasons. I hadn't mastered styling my natural hair. I was working two jobs, going to college, paying my car note, auto insurance, health insurance, and phone bill. There wasn't any money to go to the salon every month. That meant I had to do my hair myself, so the wigs became convenient. With wigs, I was able to save money and time. There are simple steps to applying a wig. All you have to do is put on a stocking cap to cover your real hair, (if not using the cap just make sure your hair is tucked away) place the wig on your head, make sure it's on well, and go about your day. That takes about two minutes. In case you didn't know, there's an intense amount of studying required for nursing school. I needed every minute I could get. Investing in wigs was the best option for me.

There was a time my cousin won some tickets to the Comedy House. She invited me and some more cousins for a night out. I didn't want to miss out on the opportunity, but I was stressing out about a nursing exam too. Well, I went to the show and took my note cards with me to study. While the comedian was telling jokes, I was still studying.

Wigs are very versatile. I could switch the styles whenever I wanted. The main color of my wigs were black. I got them from the Asian hair store and the *Especially Yours* catalog. The styles varied from a short bob, a thick curly and bouncy wig like Oprah, a short, curly afro, a short stringy coiled wig, a layered flipped wig with a bang, and my favorite, a sassy short spiked brown wig.

During my wig phase, I'll say I was indeed an influencer. That's the term that's pretty prevalent these days. While working at the hospital, I had a cancer patient who was impressed with my hair. I was honest with her and told her it was a wig; she was shocked. She asked me where I got it from. When I told her about the store, she was excited. It was like she had hopes of feeling attractive again. She had been keeping her hair tied in head wraps. It felt good knowing that I was able to improve someone's day, just by showing up in my wig. By the way, she was a white woman.

Other influential instances include my Aunt Dee. Aunt Dee worked at the hospital as I did. She'd compliment me on my natural hair. She stopped with relaxers also and got hooked on wearing wigs after seeing me have fun with mine.

Straightening

Another style that I'd get was a press and curl or hot comb. Both are very similar. If you remember those "night before Easter" social media memes, you've seen the hot comb. If you're getting a press and curl or hair straightened with the hot comb, you will need some grease. Back in the day, the common greases (pomade) used were Dax, Royal Crown Dressing, or Blue Magic. Dax was green-colored and in a glass jar with a blue lid. I remember that Dax jar well. My great-grandma used to use it on her hair. Royal Crown Dressing was clear-colored in a paper container that resembled a paper towel roll. It had a silver-colored lid. Blue Magic was definitely blue in color; however, sometimes you could find it in green. Both were in a plastic container with a white lid. I remember my mom buying these hair greases from Walmart and Maxway.

Here's the straightening process. The hot comb which is made of iron at the top (comb) with a wooden handle is heated. If straightening is done in the home, it's heated on the stovetop. If it's done at the salon, there was a special heating tool. Before using the straightening comb, the hair grease is applied to the hair. The stylist then places the hot comb onto the root of the hair and combs it to the end. With the press and curl, a curling tool is used instead of a comb. The worst part of straightening is getting your skin burned. It's not a 3rd-degree burn, but nonetheless, a burn is a burn. Common burned skin areas are near the edges, ears, and the nape of your neck. Old folks refer to the nape as the "kitchen". Many older Black women hairstylists specialize in straightening hair.

I'd get my hair straightened just to have a different style and to see how long my hair really was. I highly recommend letting a professional straighten your hair. Believe it or not, I tried straightening my hair on my own, so I purchased an electric hot comb. This method allowed me to control the temperature of the heating element. It straightened my hair, but not like the old-fashioned hot comb. The straightening may have lasted one day before getting poofy. The other thing I tried was the flat iron. It's an electric device also. It's like a big clamp where you place your hair between a metal iron, clamp it, and pull the hair through. There is also the blowout that's popular today. When using any type of heat, you have to be careful because too much heat can damage the hair. Damage can include split ends and/or hair loss.

Braids & Twists

I'd also get protective braided styles whether it was cornrows or individual braids. When I got Kinky twists, Senegalese twists, or Nubian twists, they were done by the African braiders. These styles were really popular in the early 2000s. It cost me about $180.00 and 12-18 hours of my time. I'd keep those styles for at least 2 months.

Sometimes I'd get my mom to cornrow my hair with hair extensions. Then I'd get my cousin or aunt to do my micro braids. For the micro braids I'd go to the beauty supply store and purchase 3-4 packs of wet and wavy human hair. A decent quality pack was about $17.00. Once the micro braids were completed, I'd wet them with water or LottaBody setting lotion to give it that wet and wavy look. I used to wear this style very frequently. It was definitely a favorite. Around 2010 my cousin Viviana would do Kinky twists for me. She did my hair in the picture below. My mother, cousin, nor aunt were professional hair braiders, but if they were available, I'd let them do my hair. It saved me some money for sure.

Two-Strand Twists

Two-strand twists and twist-outs were the first natural styles that I did myself. It's literally parting your hair and taking two sections of hair and twisting the hair around each other. I did them in medium sizes initially. The first time I did it, it wasn't cute at all. Oh well, I tried. But honey when I got it right, it was cute! I just had to keep trying and experimenting with different products. As I got more comfortable, I did them in smaller sizes. I'd let the hair stay twisted for 2 weeks max. Then I'd unloosen them to create what is called the twist-out style.

Let me tell you a story about me and my twist-out style. I worked a 12-hour night shift at the hospital. I had plans to attend a wedding the next day. To save time on my hair, I wore two-strand twists to work. On the day of the wedding, I'd plan to wear the twist-out style. When I got ready around noon, I started loosening the twists. The strands would hang near my cheekbones. I just knew I was cute. The ceremony was held at a church. I can vividly recall the wedding reception held on the beach at Seabrook Island, South Carolina. As my family and I were sitting outside on the veranda overlooking the Atlantic Ocean, the moisture turned my beautiful twist-out into a teeny weeny afro (TWA). I was so mad! I learned the hard way that extreme moisture will ruin your hairstyle. I saw it for myself when I went to the bathroom. Well, all I could do is try to shape it and make it look decent.

C. Michelle Greene-Smalls, MSN, RN, CCM

CHAPTER 6

Loc Myths

Before growing my locs, I heard a few unflattering things about dreads/locs. People surely had their stereotypes about them. Here are some that I will debunk.

Myth: Dreads/locs aren't clean.
Truth: Just like hair that's not loc'd, if you wash them then they become clean.

Myth: Beeswax is needed to start dreads/locs.
Truth: No, beeswax is not needed. It can be done with gel. Some folks even use water.

Myth: Dreads/locs are unprofessional.
Truth: They are professional. Don't let anyone tell you otherwise.

Myth: Dreads/locs are for Rastafarians.
Truth: No, it's not. It's for anyone who wants to wear that hairstyle.

Myth: Only Black people wear dreads/locs.
Truth: Other races wear dreads/locs. It may not look natural or as nice as it does on Blacks, but non-Blacks loc their hair.

Myth: It is expensive to maintain dreads/locs.
Truth: Not so. It costs the same or maybe less as if you were getting a relaxer and style every 6 weeks.

Myth: You have to do the big chop to start locs.
Truth: No, you don't have to do a big chop. It's best that your hair is free from chemicals and in its natural state.

Myth: Dreads/locs will damage your hair.
Truth: If properly maintained, your hair won't be damaged. I know of a young lady who has had locs for 20 years. They are past her waist. Her hair is intact from the roots to the tips.

Myth: You have to start from scratch if you don't want to keep your dreads/locs.
Truth: No, you don't have to cut all of your hair off. You can comb the locs out and still have hair that you can style. Even if you don't comb them out, there should be enough hair for a small afro.

CHAPTER 7

Starting the Locs

Hesitation

Again, I love having natural hair. Early on, I didn't know of too many hairstyles that I could do on my own other than two-strand twists and twist-outs. Throughout the early and mid-2000s, I was not using the internet or YouTube like I do now. Needless to say, I was ready for a new style.

Although I wanted a new style, I was unsure of what the new style would be. I was interested in starting locs, but I had a concern. In my neighborhood, there was another lady around my age who had locs and people would confuse me with her quite frequently. By the way, I didn't even think we looked alike. I don't like being compared to other people and that just ruffled my feathers. I remember vehemently saying no to locs because of the comparison. Looking back, that was very simple-minded thinking.

Again, I was hesitant about starting locs initially. I liked them, but wasn't too sure about committing to the hairstyle change. From getting the kinky twists, I had an idea of what the locs would look like on me. The truth is the more I kept getting the Kinky twists, Senegalese twists, etc., I was just wasting time. I made up my mind that by the time I turned 30 I'd have my hair loc'd. In 2011, I loc'd my hair.

When I decided to loc, I felt that my hair was long enough. The back of my hair was a little past my shoulders once it was straightened or when I pulled it. Therefore, I figured I was good to go. I wouldn't start the loc journey with short hair. Don't get me wrong, there's nothing wrong with that, but it just didn't go well with my plans. And I plan everything!

Coiled Locs

I found a natural hair stylist who had an appointment available to start my locs. I chose the coil method versus the two-strand twists. The coil method is where a fine-tooth comb is used and the hair is twisted to the left or right in a spiral from the roots to the end. The two-strand twist is just that. Taking strands of the hair, dividing it into two sections, and twisting the hair together like an overlap. Eventually, the hairs will intertwine together. Also with the coils, the stylist used the palm roll method to coil the hair. It smoothes the loose hairs in the coils too. Palm rolling is when the hair is saturated with a liquid and glides between the palm of your hands which causes the hair to roll.

Depending on your hair type by mouth two, your hair may begin to loc. You will start to see and feel your hair intertwine and become hard. The hair (loc) won't look the same way it started. This is called the budding phase.

Additional Types of Locs

Other locs that you can get are Sisterlocs. They are super duper tiny. It looks like five strands of hair intertwined together. The Sisterlocs look like tiny strings. They can cost up to $1,000.00 to get installed. Plus, it could take several hours to complete. Personally, I like this look on older, seasoned women.

Microlocs are very small individual locs, closely resembling Sisterlocs. Like Sisterlocs, the microlocs create more volume of hair.

The So-Called Ugly Phase

Many people refer to the ugly phase as when you first start your locs. It's when the locs are short. I didn't know the "ugly phase" was a thing at the time I was getting my locs. Having short hair isn't ugly at all. That's just not what I had planned. Another thing that I didn't know was that my hair was going to shrink! I figured since my hair was shoulder length when straightened, I'd have locs with some length. Well, that didn't happen at all. My hair was two to three times as short. I worried about having short hair due to my body type. I was skinny with small breasts, so my biggest fear was being mistaken for a guy. In order to compensate, I wore fitted clothing, particularly tops and dangling earrings.

Hang Time

When your hair starts to get longer, some people refer to it as "hang time". Just another term for length. Everyone's hair growth is different. By year two, I definitely had hair touching my shoulders.

See the picture below. The length of your locs will be down your back eventually if you maintain them properly.

CHAPTER 8

Loc Maintenance Routine

I went to the stylist once a month initially. Here I'd get my hair shampooed, conditioned, retwisted, and styled. I'm just going to let you know now that you're encouraged not to wash your hair frequently during the first few months of starting your locs. Sounds crazy right? The reason for that is because frequent washing will prevent the hair from loc'ing.

Here's what I did as a substitute for washing my hair. In between my stylist visits, I'd use a waterless shampoo. I bought it at a local pharmacy in the ethnic hair section. The shampoo was in a spray bottle. I just sprayed it on my scalp, took a damp cloth, and rubbed it across my scalp. Then I was done.

Shampoos & Conditioners

When getting my hair shampooed by the stylist, I let the stylist use whatever she was using at the salon. When I was shampooing my hair on my own, I didn't use any shampoos or conditioners that contained sulfates. Sulfates are used in detergents. I didn't want that type of chemical on my hair. I'm big on reading product ingredients. My goal was to avoid products with long-named ingredients that I couldn't identify. I tried natural brands like Jason, Shea Moisture, and others that I found at Whole Foods Market.

When shampooing and conditioning the locs, I made sure all areas of my hair were lathered very well. I cleansed my scalp and all the locs from the root to the end. I then used warm water to rinse the lather out. Typically, I washed and rinsed my hair in the kitchen sink. Once my hair became really long, rinsing the locs while showering was better at ensuring that all of the lather got rinsed out.

As my hair became longer and fuller, shampooing it became a little challenging. On my wash days, sometimes I'd part my hair into four sections and shampooed the locs. This helped me to know for sure that I was getting all of the locs cleaned. I generally shampooed my hair once or twice a month. If I've been working out and my hair was drenched in sweat, I'd shampoo my hair again.

While conditioning my hair, if the bottle of conditioner said to leave on the hair for 5 minutes, I'd leave it on for 15-30 minutes, cover with a plastic bag or shower cap, and then rinse it out. Here's why. It takes 5 minutes or more to apply the conditioner, so in my opinion, that's not enough time. Generally while conditioning my hair I'd get distracted, so the conditioner usually stayed on for 30 minutes.

Deep Cleansing Rinse

Over time you will accumulate product build-up, lint, ketchup, etc. in your hair. Sometimes it's visible and sometimes it's not. Every few months or so, after a shampoo I'd do a deep cleansing rinse on my locs. I started doing this when my locs were down my back. That's just when I learned about it. I'm sure you can do it sooner, perhaps at shoulder length. I recommend shoulder length because I can't imagine short hair being able to flow freely in a water filled sink or basin.

When deep cleansing, I'd combine apple cider vinegar, baking soda, and lemon juice into warm water in the sink. The water would begin as a light tan color. I'd place my long hair in the sink for about 10 minutes for deep cleaning. Once done, the water became dark brown and murky. After removing my hair from the murky water, I'd give my hair a final rinse.

Don't do this when you are just starting your locs. Remember you don't want them becoming saturated early on. It will prevent the hair from loc'ing correctly.

Retwists

As your hair grows over time, the locs unravel at the base (roots). Retwisting provides a neat look for the locs. An important thing to note is to make sure you or your stylist is retwisting the loc in the same direction that the loc was started. It helps to maintain the initial pattern of the loc.

Retwisting is generally done after washing the hair. It's done by applying gel (typically Eco gel) at the roots and twisting the hair to the left or right via palm rolling. Then a metal hair clip is attached to the loc to help keep the newly twisted loc in place. After the clip is secured in the hair, it's time to sit under the hair dryer. A stylist will have you sit under the dryer for what seems like forever. It's usually 30 minutes or more.

Initially, I was stuck on having a neat look. I always wanted my hair retwisted as soon as possible. Typically my hair was retwisted at least once a month by the stylist. In between times, I'd retwist my hair myself. As my hair grew past my shoulders I wasn't concerned with retwisting. There were times when I went a few months not retwisting my hair. Boy was my hair thick! My scalp was not visible at all. Although my hair wasn't retwisted, my hair never looked unkempt or unhealthy.

Interlocking

This is an alternative method to retwisting. I've never had this done on my hair, although I've seen it done. It's where a crochet hook and needle are used to tighten the hair at the base by partially separating the "new growth" and bringing the end of the loc between the separated new growth. It can be done multiple times to your level of satisfaction.

Moisturizing LOC Method

Moisturizing your locs is important. You can decide how often you want to moisturize your hair. If you choose not to use the LOC method, I recommend at least spraying water on your hair. That can be done daily or as often you choose.

I learned about the LOC method late in loc life. I mean probably by my fifth year. I didn't have a stylist tell me about it. One day on Pinterest I saw information about it in my newsfeed. LOC is an acronym for liquid, oil, and conditioner. When maintaining your locs, you should apply this method to seal the moisture in your hair.

Liquid should be water-based. I typically use tap water that I place in a bottle and spray onto my hair. You can also use a leave-in conditioner.

Oil should be applied next. Oils provide shine and moisture to your hair. My preference is plain natural oils. Apply the oil to your damp hair. You can use oils like coconut, grapeseed, carrot seed, olive oil, argan oil, and jojoba oil. These are considered lightweight oils. The oils also have a light texture. I just recently tried avocado oil. It's also a lightweight oil and it feels light. Moroccan oil and Jamaican black castor oil feels heavy, so I'll say it's a heavyweight oil.

I'd take the oil from the bottle and pour it in my hand and apply it to my hair. If the oil was available in a spray bottle, I'd just spray it directly onto the hair. Another method I'd use was placing the oils directly onto my scalp. I found a cone-shaped top to attach to my oil bottle. It had a small opening and I used it to apply the oil directly onto my scalp.

Coconut oil became my friend. I used it frequently. Sometimes I'd switch it up and use argan oil, grapeseed oil, and Moroccan oil. You may think those are expensive, but sometimes I'd also use the cheaper oils that you find at Walmart that contained olive oil or carrot seed oil like Palmer's and African Pride from time to time.

My hair truly sucks up moisture. I could apply oils and creams to my hair and it would still look dry. I got fed up one day. Let me tell you a story. I was at work, sitting at my desk. I was new to the department and it was picture day. When I got my picture back my face was so greasy! Well, what happened was, I decided to put so much oil on my hair, that whatever didn't get absorbed started dripping on my face and down my neck. You'd think I ran 2 miles and then took a picture. I was still cute though.

I'm sure you've heard of the phrase "greasing your scalp". I'd do this at least once a week before my locs and with my locs. Greasing your scalp is a method of applying oil to your hair. Essentially you are just applying hair grease or pomade to the roots of your hair. Remember your hair grows from the root so you want to keep it nourished.

When it comes to oils, I don't use any products that have petroleum or petrolatum in them. This ingredient clogs your pores.

Cream or Leave-In Conditioner application is the last step. This can be a butter base or creamy moisturizer. This will help seal the oil into your hair.

Hair Protection

I recommend that you cover your hair while you sleep. I sleep with my hair covered. You can use a bonnet, scarf, or a wrap. If you have your hair styled, the scarf will protect your style. It will also prevent lint from collecting in your hair.

The covering can be made of satin, silk, polyester, or a combination of fabrics. Typically the coverings are inexpensive. They can be purchased from Walmart, Dollar General, Amazon, etc.

CHAPTER 9

Interesting Things I Didn't Know Before Starting Locs

Hair Shrinkage

I thought if my natural hair was touching my shoulders I'd start with long locs. Nope! Your hair will shrink and become super short.

Hair Washing

There's no frequent washing of the locs initially. If so, the locs won't have a great chance at actually loc'ing. Before the locs, I was washing my natural hair every two weeks.

Combing Out the Locs

You can comb your hair out. Yes, this is an option! It doesn't matter if you're in the early or late phase. My cousin has done it multiple times in the early phase. I saw a stylist do it for her client, and I even combed out a few very old locs of my own.

Combing out the locs is a long process in my experience. It took me one hour to comb out one loc. It was exhausting. If you're going to do it, it requires patience. You need to really wet the loc and use a fine-tooth comb. I started at the bottom of the loc and worked my way to the top. Keep in mind that you will lose hair so don't be surprised. However, I was surprised that the hair that I combed from the loc was as long as the loc.

Marrying the Locs

When I heard this phrase, I looked confused. Marrying the locs simply means combining two or more locs together so they will grow as one. Typically the locs will be within proximity of each other then retwisted at the base. Over a short duration, the locs will intertwine together.

In my case I had some thinning locs, so my stylist married a few locs. With the size of my locs, it was unnoticeable that some of my locs were married.

Loc Reattachment

Did you know that if you ever decided to cut your locs off you could get them reattached? Well, you sure can! Just save those locs and make sure they are clean. Then you will be able to do so.

Here's what I did. I cut my locs off because I wanted a new style. I saved the locs that were cut. At the time, I wasn't sure what I was going to do with them. A few years passed and I decided that I wanted to add them back to my hair.

I let my hair grow back and contacted a professional loctician. She required that my hair be at least three inches long. It was definitely at least that. Before the loc reattaching could begin, the loctician requested that I bring in the old locs so she could clean them. The actual methods of reattaching varies. The loctician plaited my hair and then added the kinky textured hair extensions to it. Then voila! My head was full of locs again.

CHAPTER 10

Mistakes With My Locs

Size

I didn't want to have small locs, so I requested a medium size. In my opinion, what I got wasn't medium locs. They were quite small to me. My recommendation for you is to have a picture of what you want if going to a stylist.

Stylist Portfolio

When looking for a stylist, don't just take someone's word that they do locs. Ask for pictures of their work. When I started with my locs, I was only on one social media platform, which was Facebook. Today, I'm on Instagram as well. Many stylists share their work on Instagram, Facebook, Snapchat, TikTok, etc. I said all of that to say, today there's no excuse not to see anyone's work.

Adding Color

I told my stylist I wanted to try some color. I made sure that she understood that I didn't want anything permanent because I didn't like the colored tip look. She said she was going to do a rinse. A rinse is temporary, she said. With a rinse, the color would come out in a few weeks. Sounded good to me.

Well, weeks passed and the color was still there. At this point, I figured the stylist wasn't honest with me. I went to my secondary stylist and she confirmed that it was a permanent dye in my hair. I was devastated because I told that chic I didn't want anything permanent. Again, I was stuck with this decision. The lesson here is if you want to try something new to your hair, get a second opinion from a different professional.

Leave-in Conditioners

I was never big on leave-in conditioners. I was so used to leaving the conditioner on my hair and rinsing it out afterward. You want a leave-in conditioner to maintain moisture in your hair. It also softens the hair and keeps it from looking dull. I should've been using a leave-in conditioner early on in my loc process.

Experienced Loctician

When I first got my locs, I trusted the owner of the salon, thinking I was going to get her when I booked my appointment. Instead, I got a stylist who was just starting. I get it, everyone has to start somewhere. She kept referring to the owner with questions. That's how I knew she was a newbie. Since I was already in the chair, I figured it would be okay under the owner's tutelage. The lesson here is to get the person that you know you want.

Another thing I want to point out is that a true loctician knows what he or she is doing. If you have any inkling that something isn't right, trust your gut. So here's what happened. I needed a new stylist who specialized in locs after my initial loctician and I parted ways. I have a family member who had locs. Therefore, I thought, perhaps I can go to whomever he's going to. Well, I got his stylist's number and started going to her. That didn't last too long either. Here are the red flags that I ignored.

Flag #1

The new stylist wanted to trim my locs! I never heard of such a thing! Being new, I was like well okay, trusting that she knew what she was doing. Wrong! Here's what happened. The locs were a little frayed, so she was trimming them to look neat. Well by a week or so I noticed a few locs had gotten super duper thin in the middle of the locs. It took me a while to figure it out, but that was the only logical reason.

Flag #2

I brought the thin loc to the stylist's attention. She had a solution for that. Her solution was to just loop that loc into a knot! Sounds crazy, right? Me believing that she knew her stuff, I let her do it. Well as the hair grew, that loc started looking crazy. As it began to grow, it grew at an angle and not vertically. As time continued to pass, I was upset about letting her do that to my hair.

Flag #3

As a licensed cosmetologist, you'd think hair washing is a basic skill. As she was shampooing my hair, I noticed she wasn't washing the ends of my hair. Well, the same stylist told me that you don't have to wash the ends with locs. I'm replaying in my head like, "How can that be?" Being naive and thinking she knows more than I did, I went along with it, until I started going to another salon.

Flag #4

I like the curly look. I was starting to get some hang time and was ready for new styles, particularly up-dos. Don't you know homegirl took an iron curler in an attempt to curl my locs! She swore that was possible and that it was fine. Well, she tried a few locs and it didn't work. I wondered why. Matter of fact, I know why. It's because you don't need a curling iron to curl locs!

Flag #5

Like I said before, I like curls. Back then I'd curl my hair, but have her shampoo, condition, and retwist. After my salon visit, I'd go home and curl my hair with pipe cleaners (Fuzzy Sticks that can be found in the craft section of Walmart). I did a great job, might I add.

One day I told the stylist that I was going to curl my hair when I got home. She never curled my hair before, but she insisted she could do it for me with her rollers. I asked if she had done it before. Of course, she replied yes, but that could've been a lie. I figured if I let her do it, it would save me some time. Well, that was an epic fail! The hair was barely curled after sitting under the dryer for what seemed to be an eternity. The curls weren't even worth paying for. She was pleased with it and I was not. I told her when I do it, it looks better. I knew our time together was going to come to an end.

CHAPTER 11

Loc Acceptance

Loc Influencer

Remember I told you about me being an influencer with my natural hair. Well it didn't stop there. Once I got my locs my family did too. Particularly on my mother's side. I started another revolution. My loc journey began in early 2011. Around Christmas 2011, I invited the family to my house for dinner. I was the only one loc'd. I wasn't recruiting for #TeamLocs, but sure enough by 2012 the roster was filling up. My cousin Talia started her locs that year. Then my younger cousin Keshara started hers. She was still in elementary school. I was amazed that she wanted to loc her hair at such a young age. However, on the other hand, I never saw locs on anyone when I was her age. The person who shocked me the most was my granduncle MJ. He's a seasoned, old-school guy. Once he retired, he said he was going to loc his hair. And that's what he did. All of us who were loc'd would gather around at family gatherings and talk all things loc'd from hair products, styles, maintenance, etc. It's like we were a family within a family when it came to locs. Unc called us radical. We definitely went against the family norm with the loc'd hair.

Crown Act

Have you ever wondered if your natural hair would be deemed acceptable in the workplace?

Before I started loc'ing my hair, I wondered if it would be considered professional or non-professional. Since I've started the natural hair process, I've held a job in the hospital. When I decided to begin locs, I questioned whether it was a professional look. In the early 2000s at the first hospital, where I worked, I only saw one woman with locs. She was older than me, plus she worked in the lab. I didn't see any doctors, nurses, therapists, or any other bedside employees with locs. Basically, what I'm saying is, I rarely saw locs in the professional setting. That also included when I moved to a bigger city and bigger hospital. Since I didn't see many professionals wearing locs, I wasn't sure how locs would be perceived. I didn't need anyone to make the decision for me to begin my locs. By the time I was really ready to start my locs, it didn't matter who had them or not. I was doing it because I wanted to. If it was going to be a problem (which it shouldn't have) I'd deal with it at that time. I'd never been approached by anyone from Human Resources or had anyone complain about my hair. Meanwhile, I was still able to get multiple jobs despite having locs. Luckily, I didn't experience hair discrimination.

There are some people who have been discriminated against for having their hair in locs. I heard about different stories on the news about how women weren't promoted because of their hairstyle or were told they had to remove their locs to keep their job. Within recent years, you may remember the young Black wrestling student who had his locs literally cut from his head in order to compete in the competition! His locs were deemed inappropriate. The ability to graduate for another young Black student in Texas was in jeopardy because the school said his locs were violating the dress code due to the length of his hair. Why are there rules about our hair in particular? I believe it's a sense of control by those who don't look like us. Those who don't have the same skin color and hair texture as we do.

Speaking of such, do you know about the Crown Act? According to thecrownact.com, it's an acronym for Creating a Respectful and Open World for Natural Hair. The Crown Act was created by the Crown Coalition. The CROWN Act's mission is to eradicate hair discrimination by making hair-based discrimination illegal.

Currently, the state of Nevada is the latest state to pass the CROWN Act. Other states include New York, New Jersey, Delaware, Connecticut, Maryland, Colorado, Nebraska, Washington, and Virginia. California was the first state to pass the Crown Act. It was introduced by Senator Holly Mitchell in 2019.

The most recent bill states:

"Creating a Respectful and Open World for Natural Hair Act of 2021 or the CROWN Act of 2021

This bill prohibits discrimination based on a person's hair texture or hairstyle if that style or texture is commonly associated with a particular race or national origin. Specifically, the bill prohibits this type of discrimination against those participating in federally assisted programs, housing programs, public accommodations, and employment.

Persons shall not be deprived of equal rights under the law and shall not be subjected to prohibited practices based on their hair texture or style." (Congress.gov)

National and International Pageants

2019 was the year for Black women in pageantry. Miss USA, Cheslie Kryst - Black. Miss Teen USA, Kaleigh Garris - Black. Miss America, Nia Franklin - Black. Miss World, Toni-Ann Singh - Black. She's from Jamaica. And I will never forget Miss Universe, Zozibini Tunzi. She's from South Africa. She has milk chocolate skin and a very short natural hairstyle. In her acceptance speech, she said she chose to wear her hair like that so children can see themselves when they see her.

That's a lot of Black beauty! I'm so proud.

Miss Locs Pageant

In 2019 I entered a pageant for women with locs. The pageant was held in Florence, South Carolina. I loved my hair and I wanted to share that same love with others. Have I ever been in a pageant before? No. Have I ever participated in a showcase? No. Nevertheless, I put my inexperience aside and went for it. I was so glad that I did.

During the pageant, contestants were judged based on talent, fashion, and Q&A. I was confident all day. I held my head up high as my locs bounced up and down while I strolled down the aisles. My responses to the Q&A were articulated very well. As I was performing my talent of wreath making, I wore my beret to show my personal style. In addition, it kept my hair out of the way. I forgot to mention, my makeup was gorgeous.

Well, I didn't win 1st, 2nd, or 3rd place. That was disappointing. There was a rush to vacate the building as the event came to an end. I was glad because that prevented me from having a self-pity party. What made my night was when a lovely little girl who may have been around 10 years old came up to me and asked to take a picture with me. In my mind, I was like, "really, me?" Maybe I inspired her. At that moment, I knew that's what being in the pageant was all about.

As I left the pageant, I recalled the famous Latin phrase, "veni, vidi, vici" meaning "I came, I saw, I conquered." Fear was conquered. People's thoughts weren't on my mind, nor was I nervous the entire day. I tried something new and did what I sought out to do even though I didn't win. I owed the experience to my younger self. The unattractive little girl with the relaxed, but still nappy hair who never thought she was pretty. The girl who was only described as smart. She's now a grown woman embracing everything about herself from her nappy crown down to her painted toes, even the crooked great toe. Today, this woman is not only smart, she's creative, talented, naturally pretty, and beautiful inside and out.

CHAPTER 12

Easy Do It Yourself (DIY) Styles

I love the versatility of various styles that you can do with locs. I've styled my hair on a whim several times. My go-to styles are crimps and curls. I'll share with you some styles I've done.

Side Swoop
This is the simplest style ever whether your locs are straight, crimpy, or curly. There are two ways to do this:
1) Bring the front part of your hair upward and over to the right side or vice versa. You may want to use Bobby pins or a clip to help hold some locs in place.
2) Have all of your hair hang as normal. Then swoop it to the right side of your neck or vice versa.

Quit Making Excuses & Loc Your Hair

Ponytail

You can pull the hair up in the top, pull it back, or on the side. You can tie it with a scrunchie or stretchy headband depending upon the amount of hair that you have.

Here I am with my hair in a side ponytail. I used my own loc to gather the ponytail.

Upward Fish Tail

Gather your hair from the back to the front then French braid the hair. Tuck or pin the tip of the braid underneath the French braid near your forehead.

High Bun

Use your ponytail holder and make a ponytail. Once it is snug enough to your comfort level, keep the hair in a ball instead of releasing it for an actual ponytail. If you have a lot of hair, you may have to get creative and tuck the locs to complete the bun look.

Messy Bun

Pull your hair up into a ponytail. This time don't worry about having all of your hair neatly placed into the ponytail. It can be loose. Instead of releasing the hair, keep it in a bun. It's perfectly fine to have hair hanging from the bun. Hence the term "messy".

Twisted Bun

Pull your hair up into a ponytail. Take a few locs and twist them as if you were doing a two-strand twist. Then take the twisted locs and pin them in the form of a tight loop.

Curls

Curls can be achieved multiple ways with pipe cleaners also known as Fuzzy Sticks, spongy curlers, or any other loc curling tool. I tend to curl 2-4 locs at a time. Take the curling tool and loop the tool at the tip near the root of the hair. Then begin to wrap the hair around the tool. Once you're at the end, fold the tool to secure all of the hairs. The curls will be more defined if the hair is wet first.

Curling Tool Style

Sometimes I wear the curling tools in public, too. If it looks cute, I'm rocking it. Wearing the curling tools allowed me to have a short style, although my hair was long.

Crimps

Crimps are so beautiful. You can do it with short or long locs. First, wet your hair with water. Then braid (plait) your hair into small sections. Considering the length of my locs, I'd use at least 6-9 locs for my plait. Sometimes the braid isn't completely unified at the end. If this happens you can use a rubber band to contain the hairs in the braid to prevent it from unraveling.

You'll have better results the longer you leave the braid in. I suggest if you braid it at night, to loosen the braid the next day. This style will last only a few days.

Halo Braid

Start a French braid from one side of your head near your ear. Then continue the braid around your head. Secure the end of the braid with a rubber band. Tuck or pin the end of the braid into a non-visible part of halo braid.

Bantu Knots

Divide your hair into sections. The amount of sections depends on how many knots you desire. Gather a few locs and begin to two-strand twist them. At the end of the twist, use a rubber band to maintain the twists. At the top of the twist, make a small downward fold, then begin to wrap the hair in a clockwise motion. Lastly, secure the Bantu knot with Bobby pins.

Afterword

Thank you for taking the time to read this book. I hope you enjoyed it as much as I did writing it. It is also my hope that you find the book to be helpful wherever you are on your loc journey.

Let's connect! Follow me here:

Instagram: Succeeding Naturally
Website: Succeedingnaturally.com
Facebook: Succeeding Naturally - Blog

About the Author

C. Michelle Greene-Smalls, MSN, RN, CCM, was raised in Mayesville, South Carolina. It is the birthplace of Dr. Mary McLeod Bethune. Michelle is a wife and plant mom. She's a full-time registered nurse with a master's degree in nursing education. One of her most recent accomplishments include being recognized as South Carolina Black Pages Top 20 Under 40 in 2019. The retail company, New York & Company, featured Michelle on their social media pages in 2020. She volunteers in her community and is an active member of her church. Her hobbies include traveling, playing word games, and crafting.

Michelle had the desire to become an author as a young girl in elementary school. This is her first publication. In this book, she hopes that Black women feel encouraged to embrace their natural hair, start their locs, and let go of any perceptions that could hinder them from their loc journey.

www.ingramcontent.com/pod-product-compliance
Lightning Source LLC
Chambersburg PA
CBHW070335120526
44590CB00017B/2887